Sweet and Bitter Bark

. . .

Selected Poems by Robert Frost

The Nature Company Classics

The Nature Company owes its vision to the world's great naturalists: Charles Darwin, Henry David Thoreau, John Muir, David Brower, Rachel Carson, Jacques Cousteau, and many others. Through their inspiration, we are dedicated to providing products and experiences which encourage the joyous observation, understanding, and appreciation of nature. We do not advocate, and will not allow to be sold in our stores, any products which result from the killing of wild animals for trophy purposes. Seashells, butterflies, furs, and mounted animal specimens fall into this category. Our goal is to provide you with products, insights, and experiences which kindle your own sense of wonder and which help you to feel good about yourself and the world in which you live.

Edited by Catherine Gudis, Los Angeles
Designed by Jacqueline Jones Design, San Francisco

Produced by Mandarin Offset
Printed and bound in Hong Kong

Fifth Printing

Frontispiece: Vincent van Gogh, *Irises* (detail), 1889
Table of Contents: Vincent van Gogh, *Undergrowth with Two Figures* (detail), 1890
Slipcase cover: Bernard Perlin, *The Farewell* (detail), 1952;
Albert Renger-Patzsch, *Buchenwald im Herbst*, 1936 (inset)

Joseph Raphael, *Holland Tulip Fields* (detail), 1913

Contents

Introduction

Considered one of the greatest and most influential twentieth-century American poets, Robert Frost is beloved by people of all ages and generations. Although at the root of his poetry is a deep-seated desire to explore the complex meaning of life in the modern world, some of the most significant aspects of Frost's work as a whole are his uses of natural imagery and pastoral narratives. In his poems, Frost escapes to the immensity of the natural landscape, withdrawing to a wilderness where the true essence of existence and order of life can be located. For Frost, nature is a source of peace and healing, the place — be it in the woods, by a brook, or under an azure sky — where the full range of human emotions may be experienced and the majesty of the universe unfolded.

The poems collected in *Sweet and Bitter Bark* suggest the breadth of Frost's explorations of nature — from his most direct, spontaneous observations to his most poignant and bittersweet recollections. They are selected from early volumes of poetry written while Frost lived and worked (as a farmer as well as a poet and a teacher) in the countryside of New Hampshire and England, and evidence the influence of that landscape on Frost. Frost's symbols and pastoral images originate in this lay of the land, while his simple and straightforward use of language is reminiscent of the New England heritage. In his poetry, Frost acts as a guide to the natural environment in two ways, as observer — realistically rendering the landscape — and as poet-muse — evoking nostalgic memories through dramatizations of everyday natural occurrences. Evident in both, however, is Frost's conception of nature as precious, mutable, and transcendent.

Frost's eloquent depictions of nature are brought together in *Sweet and Bitter Bark* with a rich and provocative selection of paintings, photographs, and drawings. Accompanying the poems as well as comprising a catalogue of plates in the latter portion of the book, the artworks are not intended to be directly or literally illustrative. Rather, they evoke the natural environments and intimate emotions explored by Frost in his poetry and provide another means by which to interpret the natural landscape. Spanning the late nineteenth to the early and mid-twentieth-centuries, the artworks concentrate on the period roughly coinciding with the years of Frost's life. Indeed, many were created within several years of the poems they join. Focusing on exemplary works by French and American Impressionists, Fauves (or in English, "wild beasts"), and American Modernists, the selection illustrates the range and inventiveness of artistic approaches to nature, particularly regarding light, color, and atmosphere. Masterpieces of the modern era, the works are drawn from some of the finest public and private collections in the world.

Sweet and Bitter Bark is organized thematically into three chapters which trace the expanding lens of the poet's vision: "The Pasture," "Into the Woods," and "Wind, Water, and Ice." A full sweep of emotional and physical territory is covered, from intimate landscapes to remote cosmos, from the substantial to the ephemeral, from the timebound to the timeless. Following Frost's own progression in his poetry, *Sweet and Bitter Bark* ranges from expressions of delicate pastoral beauty to the amalgam of sensations experienced in the lengthened shadows of the wilderness and the infinite expanses of the celestial bodies. So, too, are the endlessly repeating cycles of life, death, and rebirth that are found in nature — and which Frost replicates within the complex schemata of his poetry — suggested by the ordering here. With this offering of poetry and art, *Sweet and Bitter Bark* strives to open the realm of creative possibilities for representing and interpreting nature.

— *Catherine Gudis, Editor*

The Pasture

ROSE POGONIAS

A saturated meadow,
　　　　Sun-shaped and jewel-small,
A circle scarcely wider
　　　　Than the trees around were tall;
Where winds were quite excluded,
　　　　And the air was stifling sweet
With the breath of many flowers —
　　　　A temple of the heat.

There we bowed us in the burning,
　　　　As the sun's right worship is,
To pick where none could miss them
　　　　A thousand orchises;
For though the grass was scattered,
　　　　Yet every second spear
Seemed tipped with wings of color,
　　　　That tinged the atmosphere.

We raised a simple prayer
　　　　Before we left the spot,
That in the general mowing
　　　　That place might be forgot;
Or if not all so favored,
　　　　Obtain such grace of hours,
That none should mow the grass there
　　　　While so confused with flowers.

Robert William Vonnoh, *Poppies* (detail), 1888

I went to turn the grass once after one
Who mowed it in the dew before the sun.

The dew was gone that made his blade so keen
Before I came to view the leveled scene.

I looked for him behind an isle of trees;
I listened for his whetstone on the breeze.

But he had gone his way, the grass all mown,
And I must be, as he had been — alone,

"As all must be," I said within my heart,
"Whether they work together or apart."

But as I said it, swift there passed me by
On noiseless wing a bewildered butterfly,

Seeking with memories grown dim o'er night
Some resting flower of yesterday's delight.

And once I marked his flight go round and round,
As where some flower lay withering on the ground.

And then he flew as far as eye could see,
And then on tremulous wing came back to me.

I thought of questions that have no reply,
And would have turned to toss the grass to dry;

But he turned first, and led my eye to look
At a tall tuft of flowers beside a brook,

A leaping tongue of bloom the scythe had spared
Beside a reedy brook the scythe had bared.

I left my place to know them by their name,
Finding them butterfly weed when I came.

The mower in the dew had loved them thus,
By leaving them to flourish, not for us,

Nor yet to draw one thought of ours to him,
But from sheer morning gladness at the brim.

The butterfly and I had lit upon,
Nevertheless, a message from the dawn,

That made me hear the wakening birds around,
And hear his long scythe whispering to the ground,

And feel a spirit kindred to my own;
So that henceforth I worked no more alone;

But glad with him, I worked as with his aid,
And weary, sought at noon with him the shade;

And dreaming, as it were, held brotherly speech
With one whose thought I had not hoped to reach.

"Men work together," I told him from the heart,
"Whether they work together or apart."

Following pages: Henry Edmond Cross, *The Artist's Garden at St. Clair* (detail), 1904–5

Something there is that doesn't love a wall,
That sends the frozen-ground-swell under it,
And spills the upper boulders in the sun;
And makes gaps even two can pass abreast.
The work of hunters is another thing:
I have come after them and made repair
Where they have left not one stone on a stone,
But they would have the rabbit out of hiding,
To please the yelping dogs. The gaps I mean,
No one has seen them made or heard them made,
But at spring mending-time we find them there.
I let my neighbor know beyond the hill;
And on a day we meet to walk the line
And set the wall between us once again.
We keep the wall between us as we go.
To each the boulders that have fallen to each.
And some are loaves and some so nearly balls
We have to use a spell to make them balance:
"Stay where you are until our backs are turned!"
We wear our fingers rough with handling them.
Oh, just another kind of outdoor game,

One on a side. It comes to little more:
There where it is we do not need the wall:
He is all pine and I am apple orchard.
My apple trees will never get across
And eat the cones under his pines, I tell him.
He only says, "Good fences make good neighbors."
Spring is the mischief in me, and I wonder
If I could put a notion in his head:
"Why do they make good neighbors? Isn't it
Where there are cows? But here there are no cows.
Before I built a wall I'd ask to know
What I was walling in or walling out,
And to whom I was like to give offense.
Something there is that doesn't love a wall,
That wants it down." I could say "Elves" to him,
But it's not elves exactly, and I'd rather
He said it for himself. I see him there,
Bringing a stone grasped firmly by the top
In each hand, like an old-stone savage armed.
He moves in darkness as it seems to me,
Not of woods only and the shade of trees.
He will not go behind his father's saying,
And he likes having thought of it so well
He says again, "Good fences make good neighbors."

Vincent van Gogh, *Houses at Anvers* (detail), 1890

A LATE WALK

When I go up through the mowing field,
     The headless aftermath,
Smooth-laid like thatch with the heavy dew,
     Half closes the garden path.

And when I come to the garden ground,
     The whir of sober birds
Up from the tangle of withered weeds
     Is sadder than any words.

A tree beside the wall stands bare,
     But a leaf that lingered brown,
Disturbed, I doubt not, by my thought,
     Comes softly rattling down.

I end not far from my going forth
     By picking the faded blue
Of the last remaining aster flower
     To carry again to you.

Edward Steichen, *Moonrise–Mamaroneck, New York*, 1904

IN A VALE

When I was young, we dwelt in a vale
      By a misty fen that rang all night,
And thus it was the maidens pale
I knew so well, whose garments trail
      Across the reeds to a window light.

The fen had every kind of bloom,
      And for every kind there was a face,
And a voice that has sounded in my room
Across the sill from the outer gloom.
      Each came singly unto her place,

But all came every night with the mist;
      And often they brought so much to say
Of things of moment to which, they wist,
One so lonely was fain to list,
      That the stars were almost faded away

Before the last went, heavy with dew,
      Back to the place from which she came —
Where the bird was before it flew,
Where the flower was before it grew,
      Where bird and flower were one and the same.

And thus it is I know so well
      Why the flower has odor, the bird has song.
You have only to ask me, and I can tell.
No, not vainly there did I dwell,
      Nor vainly listen all the night long.

Claude Monet, *Poppy Field in a Hollow near Giverny* (detail), 1885

THE VANTAGE POINT

If tired of trees I seek again mankind,
     Well I know where to hie me — in the dawn,
     To a slope where the cattle keep the lawn.
There amid lolling juniper reclined,
Myself unseen, I see in white defined
     Far off the homes of men, and farther still,
     The graves of men on an opposing hill,
Living or dead, whichever are to mind.

And if by noon I have too much of these,
     I have but to turn on my arm, and lo,
     The sunburned hillside sets my face aglow,
My breathing shakes the bluet like a breeze,
     I smell the earth, I smell the bruised plant,
     I look into the crater of the ant.

Georgia O'Keeffe, *The Red Hills with Sun (Red Hills, Lake George)* (detail), 1927

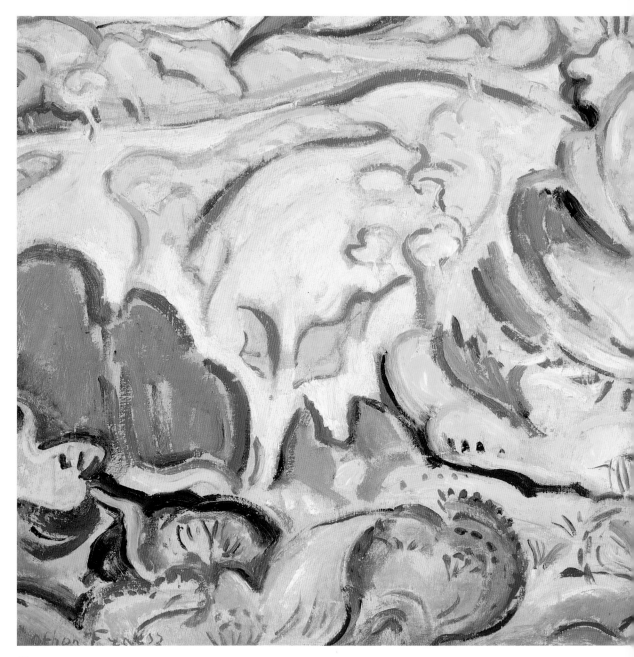

RANGE-FINDING

The battle rent a cobweb diamond-strung
And cut a flower beside a ground bird's nest
Before it stained a single human breast.
The stricken flower bent double and so hung.
And still the bird revisited her young.
A butterfly its fall had dispossessed
A moment sought in air his flower of rest,
Then lightly stooped to it and fluttering clung.

On the bare upland pasture there had spread
O'ernight 'twixt mullein stalks a wheel of thread
And straining cables wet with silver dew.
A sudden passing bullet shook it dry.
The indwelling spider ran to greet the fly,
But finding nothing, sullenly withdrew.

Othon Friesz, *Paysage* (detail), 1907

MY BUTTERFLY

Thine emulous fond flowers are dead, too,
And the daft sun-assaulter, he
That frighted thee so oft, is fled or dead:
Save only me
(Nor is it sad to thee!)
Save only me
There is none left to mourn thee in the fields.

The gray grass is scarce dappled with the snow;
Its two banks have not shut upon the river;
But it is long ago —
It seems forever —
Since first I saw thee glance,
With all the dazzling other ones,
In airy dalliance,
Precipitate in love,
Tossed, tangled, whirled and whirled above,
Like a limp rose-wreath in a fairy dance.

When that was, the soft mist
Of my regret hung not on all the land,
And I was glad for thee,
And glad for me, I wist.

Thou didst not know, who tottered, wandering on high,
That fate had made thee for the pleasure of the wind,
With those great careless wings,
Nor yet did I.

And there were other things:
It seemed God let thee flutter from his gentle clasp,
Then fearful he had let thee win
Too far beyond him to be gathered in,
Snatched thee, o'er eager, with ungentle grasp.

Ah! I remember me
How once conspiracy was rife
Against my life —
The languor of it and the dreaming fond;
Surging, the grasses dizzied me of thought,
The breeze three odors brought,
And a gem-flower waved in a wand!

Then when I was distraught
And could not speak,
Sidelong, full on my cheek,
What should that reckless zephyr fling
But the wild touch of thy dye-dusty wing!

I found that wing broken today!
For thou art dead, I said,
And the strange birds say.
I found it with the withered leaves
Under the eaves.

Alfred Stieglitz, *Equivalent* (detail), 1929

My long two-pointed ladder's sticking through a tree
Toward heaven still,
And there's a barrel that I didn't fill
Beside it, and there may be two or three
Apples I didn't pick upon some bough.
But I am done with apple-picking now.
Essence of winter sleep is on the night,
The scent of apples: I am drowsing off.
I cannot rub the strangeness from my sight
I got from looking through a pane of glass
I skimmed this morning from the drinking trough
And held against the world of hoary grass.
It melted, and I let it fall and break.
But I was well
Upon my way to sleep before it fell,
And I could tell
What form my dreaming was about to take.
Magnified apples appear and disappear,
Stem end and blossom end,
And every fleck of russet showing clear.
My instep arch not only keeps the ache,
It keeps the pressure of a ladder-round.
I feel the ladder sway as the boughs bend.
And I keep hearing from the cellar bin
The rumbling sound
Of load on load of apples coming in.

For I have had too much
Of apple-picking: I am overtired
Of the great harvest I myself desired.
There were ten thousand thousand fruit to touch,
Cherish in hand, lift down, and not let fall.
For all
That struck the earth,
No matter if not bruised or spiked with stubble,
Went surely to the cider-apple heap
As of no worth.
One can see what will trouble
This sleep of mine, whatever sleep it is.
Were he not gone,
The woodchuck could say whether it's like his
Long sleep, as I describe its coming on,
Or just some human sleep.

Vincent van Gogh, *The Flowering Orchard* (detail), 1888

PUTTING IN THE SEED

You come to fetch me from my work tonight
When supper's on the table, and we'll see
If I can leave off burying the white
Soft petals fallen from the apple tree
(Soft petals, yes, but not so barren quite,
Mingled with these, smooth bean and wrinkled pea),
And go along with you ere you lose sight
Of what you came for and become like me,
Slave to a springtime passion for the earth.
How Love burns through the Putting in the Seed
On through the watching for that early birth
When, just as the soil tarnishes with weed,
The sturdy seedling with arched body comes
Shouldering its way and shedding the earth crumbs.

Man Ray, *Hills* (detail), 1914

THE PASTURE

I'm going out to clean the pasture spring;
I'll only stop to rake the leaves away
(And wait to watch the water clear, I may):
I shan't be gone long. — You come too.

I'm going out to fetch the little calf
That's standing by the mother. It's so young,
It totters when she licks it with her tongue.
I shan't be gone long. — You come too.

Maurice de Vlaminck, *Route maraichère* (detail), 1907

Into the Woods

THE ROAD NOT TAKEN

Two roads diverged in a yellow wood,
And sorry I could not travel both
And be one traveler, long I stood
And looked down one as far as I could
To where it bent in the undergrowth;

Then took the other, as just as fair,
And having perhaps the better claim,
Because it was grassy and wanted wear;
Though as for that the passing there
Had worn them really about the same,

And both that morning equally lay
In leaves no step had trodden black.
Oh, I kept the first for another day!
Yet knowing how way leads on to way,
I doubted if I should ever come back.

I shall be telling this with a sigh
Somewhere ages and ages hence:
Two roads diverged in a wood, and I —
I took the one less traveled by,
And that has made all the difference.

Charles Burchfield, *Afternoon in the Grove* (detail), 1916

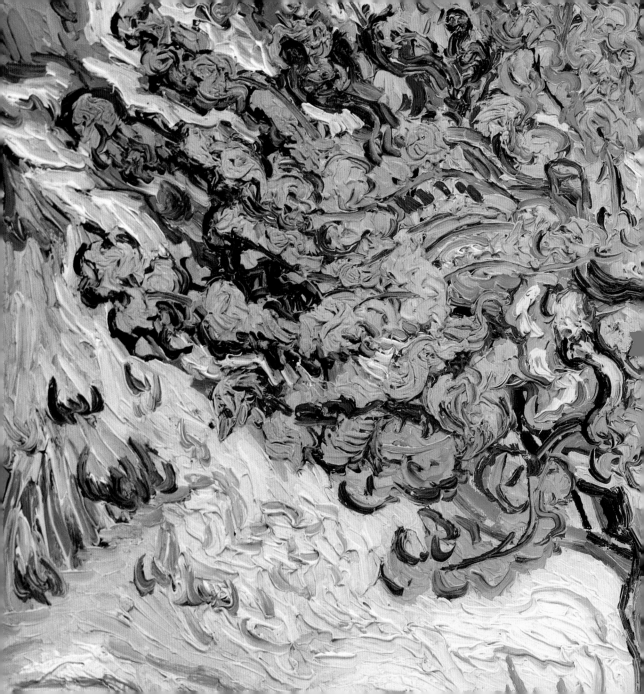

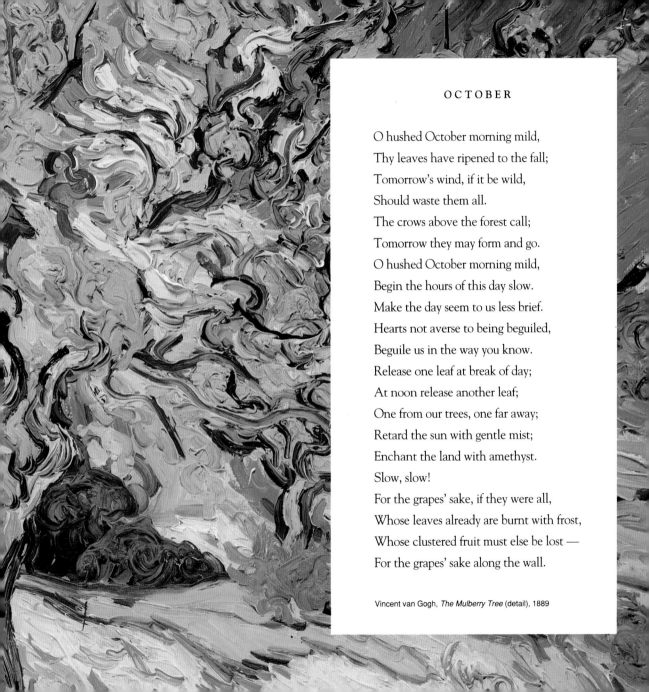

OCTOBER

O hushed October morning mild,
Thy leaves have ripened to the fall;
Tomorrow's wind, if it be wild,
Should waste them all.
The crows above the forest call;
Tomorrow they may form and go.
O hushed October morning mild,
Begin the hours of this day slow.
Make the day seem to us less brief.
Hearts not averse to being beguiled,
Beguile us in the way you know.
Release one leaf at break of day;
At noon release another leaf;
One from our trees, one far away;
Retard the sun with gentle mist;
Enchant the land with amethyst.
Slow, slow!
For the grapes' sake, if they were all,
Whose leaves already are burnt with frost,
Whose clustered fruit must else be lost —
For the grapes' sake along the wall.

Vincent van Gogh, *The Mulberry Tree* (detail), 1889

THE WOOD-PILE

Out walking in the frozen swamp one gray day,
I paused and said, "I will turn back from here.
No, I will go on farther — and we shall see."
The hard snow held me, save where now and then
One foot went down. The view was all in lines
Straight up and down of tall slim trees
Too much alike to mark or name a place by
So as to say for certain I was here
Or somewhere else: I was just far from home.
A small bird flew before me. He was careful
To put a tree between us when he lighted,
And say no word to tell me who he was
Who was so foolish as to think what he thought.
He thought that I was after him for a feather —
The white one in his tail; like the one who takes
Everything said as personal to himself.
One flight out sideways would have undeceived him.
And then there was a pile of wood for which
I forgot him and let his little fear
Carry him off the way I might have gone,
Without so much as wishing him good-night.
He went behind it to make his last stand.
It was a cord of maple, cut and split
And piled — and measured, four by four by eight.
And not another like it could I see.

No runner tracks in this year's snow looped near it.
And it was older sure than this year's cutting,
Or even last year's or the year's before.
The wood was gray and the bark warping off it
And the pile somewhat sunken. Clematis
Had wound strings round and round it like a bundle.
What held it, though, on one side was a tree
Still growing, and on one a stake and prop,
These latter about to fall. I thought that only
Someone who lived in turning to fresh tasks
Could so forget his handiwork on which
He spent himself, the labor of his ax,
And leave it there far from a useful fireplace
To warm the frozen swamp as best it could
With the slow smokeless burning of decay.

RELUCTANCE

Out through the fields and the woods
       And over the walls I have wended;
I have climbed the hills of view
       And looked at the world, and descended;
I have come by the highway home,
       And lo, it is ended.

The leaves are all dead on the ground,
       Save those that the oak is keeping
To ravel them one by one
       And let them go scraping and creeping
Out over the crusted snow,
       When others are sleeping.

And the dead leaves lie huddled and still,
       No longer blown hither and thither;
The last lone aster is gone;
       The flowers of witch hazel wither;
The heart is still aching to seek,
       But the feet question "Whither?"

Ah, when to the heart of man
       Was it ever less than a treason
To go with the drift of things,
       To yield with a grace to reason,
And bow and accept the end
       Of a love or a season?

Bernard Perlin, *The Farewell* (detail), 1952

When I see birches bend to left and right
Across the lines of straighter darker trees,
I like to think some boy's been swinging them.
But swinging doesn't bend them down to stay.
Ice storms do that. Often you must have seen them
Loaded with ice a sunny winter morning
After a rain. They click upon themselves
As the breeze rises, and turn many-colored
As the stir cracks and crazes their enamel.
Soon the sun's warmth makes them shed crystal shells
Shattering and avalanching on the snow-crust —
Such heaps of broken glass to sweep away
You'd think the inner dome of heaven had fallen.
They are dragged to the withered bracken by the load,
And they seem not to break; though once they are bowed
So low for long, they never right themselves:
You may see their trunks arching in the woods
Years afterwards, trailing their leaves on the ground
Like girls on hands and knees that throw their hair
Before them over their heads to dry in the sun.
But I was going to say when Truth broke in
With all her matter-of-fact about the ice storm
(Now am I free to be poetical?)

I should prefer to have some boy bend them
As he went out and in to fetch the cows —
Some boy too far from town to learn baseball,
Whose only play was what he found himself,
Summer or winter, and could play alone.
One by one he subdued his father's trees
By riding them down over and over again
Until he took the stiffness out of them,
And not one but hung limp, not one was left
For him to conquer. He learned all there was
To learn about not launching out too soon
And so not carrying the tree away
Clear to the ground. He always kept his poise
To the top branches, climbing carefully
With the same pains you use to fill a cup
Up to the brim, and even above the brim.
Then he flung outward, feet first, with a swish,
Kicking his way down through the air to the ground.
So was I once myself a swinger of birches.
And so I dream of going back to be.
It's when I'm weary of considerations,
And life is too much like a pathless wood
Where your face burns and tickles with the cobwebs

Broken across it, and one eye is weeping
From a twig's having lashed across it open.
I'd like to get away from earth awhile
And then come back to it and begin over.
May no fate willfully misunderstand me
And half grant what I wish and snatch me away
Not to return. Earth's the right place for love:
I don't know where it's likely to go better.
I'd like to go by climbing a birch tree,
And climb black branches up a snow-white trunk
Toward heaven, till the tree could bear no more,
But dipped its top and set me down again.
That would be good both going and coming back.
One could do worse than be a swinger of birches.

INTO MY OWN

One of my wishes is that those dark trees,
So old and firm they scarcely show the breeze,
Were not, as 'twere, the merest mask of gloom,
But stretched away unto the edge of doom.

I should not be withheld but that some day
Into their vastness I should steal away,
Fearless of ever finding open land,
Or highway where the slow wheel pours the sand.

I do not see why I should e'er turn back,
Or those should not set forth upon my track
To overtake me, who should miss me here
And long to know if still I held them dear.

They would not find me changed from him they knew —
Only more sure of all I thought was true.

Albert Renger-Patzsch, *Buchenwald im Herbst* (detail), 1936

THE OVEN BIRD

There is a singer everyone has heard,
Loud, a mid-summer and a mid-wood bird,
Who makes the solid tree trunks sound again.
He says that leaves are old and that for flowers
Mid-summer is to spring as one to ten.
He says the early petal-fall is past
When pear and cherry bloom went down in showers
On sunny days a moment overcast;
And comes that other fall we name the fall.
He says the highway dust is over all.
The bird would cease and be as other birds
But that he knows in singing not to sing.
The question that he frames in all but words
Is what to make of a diminished thing.

Thomas P. Anshutz, *Landscape* (detail), n.d.

THE SOUND OF TREES

I wonder about the trees.
Why do we wish to bear
Forever the noise of these
More than another noise
So close to our dwelling place?
We suffer them by the day
Till we lose all measure of pace,
And fixity in our joys,
And acquire a listening air.
They are that that talks of going
But never gets away;
And that talks no less for knowing,
As it grows wiser and older,
That now it means to stay.
My feet tug at the floor
And my head sways to my shoulder
Sometimes when I watch trees sway,
From the window or the door.
I shall set forth for somewhere,
I shall make the reckless choice
Some day when they are in voice
And tossing so as to scare
The white clouds over them on.
I shall have less to say,
But I shall be gone.

Charles Burchfield, *Landscape with Trees* (detail), 1915

Wind, Water, and Ice

The line-storm clouds fly tattered and swift,
  The road is forlorn all day,
Where a myriad snowy quartz stones lift,
  And the hoofprints vanish away.
The roadside flowers, too wet for the bee,
  Expend their bloom in vain.
Come over the hills and far with me,
  And be my love in the rain.

The birds have less to say for themselves
  In the wood-world's torn despair
Than now these numberless years the elves,
  Although they are no less there:
All song of woods is crushed like some
  Wild, easily shattered rose.
Come, be my love in the wet woods; come,
  Where the boughs rain when it blows.

There is the gale to urge behind
  And bruit our singing down,
And the shallow waters aflutter with wind
  From which to gather your gown.
What matter if we go clear to the west,
  And come not through dry-shod?
For wilding brooch shall wet your breast
  The rain-fresh goldenrod.

Oh, never this whelming east wind swells
  But it seems like the sea's return
To the ancient lands where it left the shells
  Before the age of the fern;
And it seems like the time when after doubt
  Our love came back amain.
Oh, come forth into the storm and rout
  And be my love in the rain.

Marsden Hartley, *Storm Clouds, Maine* (detail), 1906–7

HYLA BROOK

By June our brook's run out of song and speed.
Sought for much after that, it will be found
Either to have gone groping underground
(And taken with it all the Hyla breed
That shouted in the mist a month ago,
Like ghost of sleigh bells in a ghost of snow) —
Or flourished and come up in jewelweed,
Weak foliage that is blown upon and bent
Even against the way its waters went.
Its bed is left a faded paper sheet
Of dead leaves stuck together by the heat —
A brook to none but who remember long.
This as it will be seen is other far
Than with brooks taken otherwise in song.
We love the things we love for what they are.

André Derain, *Les Arbres* (detail), c. 1906

The well was dry beside the door,
      And so we went with pail and can
Across the fields behind the house
      To seek the brook if still it ran;

Not loth to have excuse to go,
      Because the autumn eve was fair
(Though chill), because the fields were ours,
      And by the brook our woods were there.

We ran as if to meet the moon
      That slowly dawned behind the trees,
The barren boughs without the leaves,
      Without the birds, without the breeze.

But once within the wood, we paused
      Like gnomes that hid us from the moon,
Ready to run to hiding new
      With laughter when she found us soon.

Each laid on other a staying hand
      To listen ere we dared to look,
And in the hush we joined to make
      We heard, we knew we heard the brook.

A note as from a single place,
      A slender tinkling fall that made
Now drops that floated on the pool
      Like pearls, and now a silver blade.

Wolf Kahn, *Autumn River* (detail), 1979

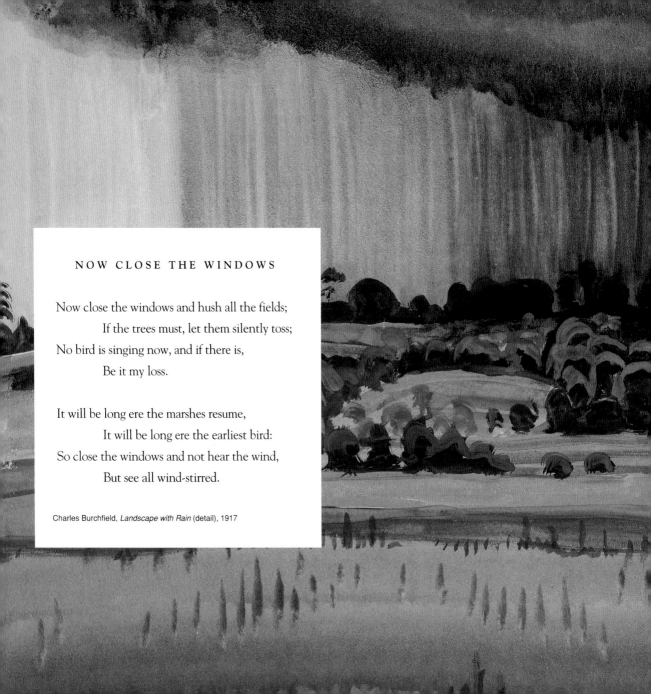

NOW CLOSE THE WINDOWS

Now close the windows and hush all the fields;
    If the trees must, let them silently toss;
No bird is singing now, and if there is,
    Be it my loss.

It will be long ere the marshes resume,
    It will be long ere the earliest bird:
So close the windows and not hear the wind,
    But see all wind-stirred.

Charles Burchfield, *Landscape with Rain* (detail), 1917

TO THE THAWING WIND

Come with rain, O loud Southwester!
Bring the singer, bring the nester;
Give the buried flower a dream;
Make the settled snowbank steam;
Find the brown beneath the white;
But whate'er you do tonight,
Bathe my window, make it flow,
Melt it as the ice will go;
Melt the glass and leave the sticks
Like a hermit's crucifix;
Burst into my narrow stall;
Swing the picture on the wall;
Run the rattling pages o'er;
Scatter poems on the floor;
Turn the poet out of door.

Arthur Dove, *Red Sun* (detail), 1935

WIND AND WINDOW FLOWER

Lovers, forget your love,
>And list to the love of these,
She a window flower,
>And he a winter breeze.

When the frosty window veil
>Was melted down at noon,
And the caged yellow bird
>Hung over her in tune,

He marked her through the pane,
>He could not help but mark,
And only passed her by,
>To come again at dark.

He was a winter wind,
>Concerned with ice and snow,
Dead weeds and unmated birds,
>And little of love could know.

But he sighed upon the sill,
>He gave the sash a shake,
As witness all within
>Who lay that night awake.

Perchance he half prevailed
>To win her for the flight
From the firelit looking-glass
>And warm stove-window light.

But the flower leaned aside
>And thought of naught to say,
And morning found the breeze
>A hundred miles away.

STARS

How countlessly they congregate
       O'er our tumultuous snow,
Which flows in shapes as tall as trees
       When wintry winds do blow! —

As if with keenness for our fate,
       Our faltering few steps on
To white rest, and a place of rest
       Invisible at dawn —

And yet with neither love nor hate,
       Those stars like some snow-white
Minerva's snow-white marble eyes
       Without the gift of sight.

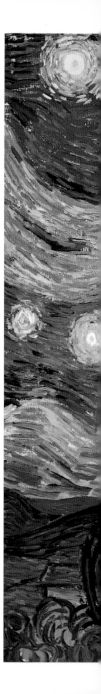

Vincent van Gogh, *The Starry Night*, 1889

Catalogue of Plates

Vincent van Gogh (Dutch, worked in France, 1853–1890). *Irises*, 1889. Oil on canvas, 28 x 36-5/8 in. (71 x 93 cm). Collection of the J. Paul Getty Museum, Malibu, California

Joseph Raphael (American, 1869–1950). *Holland Tulip Fields*, 1913. Oil on canvas, 30-1/2 x 30 in. (77.5 x 76.2 cm). Collection of the Stanford University Museum of Art. Gift of Morgan Gunst

Vincent van Gogh (Dutch, worked in France, 1853–1890). *Undergrowth with Two Figures*, 1890.
Oil on canvas, 19-3/4 x 39-1/2 in. (50 x 100 cm). Collection of the Cincinnati Art Museum.
Bequest of Mary M. Emery

Robert William Vonnoh (American, 1858–1933). *Poppies*, 1888. Oil on canvas, 13 x 18 in. (33 x 45.7 cm).
Copyright © 1992 Indianapolis Museum of Art. James E. Roberts Fund

Henry Edmond Cross (French, 1856−1910). *The Artist's Garden at St. Clair*, 1904−5. Watercolor on paper, 10-1/2 x 14 in. (26.6 x 35.8 cm). Collection of The Metropolitan Museum of Art, New York. Harris Brisbane Dick Fund.

Vincent van Gogh (Dutch, worked in France, 1853–1890). *Houses at Anvers*, 1890. Oil on canvas, 29-3/4 x 24-3/8 in. (75.5 x 61.8 cm). Collection of the Museum of Fine Arts, Boston. Bequest of John T. Spaulding, 1948

Edward Steichen (American, b. Luxembourg, 1879–1973). *Moonrise, Mamaroneck, New York*, 1904. Platinum, cyanotype, and ferro prussiate print, 15-15/16 x 19 in. (40.5 x 48.3 cm). Collection, The Museum of Modern Art, New York. Gift of the photographer. Reprinted with the permission of Joanna T. Steichen

Claude Monet (French, 1840–1926). *Poppy Field in a Hollow near Giverny*, 1885. Oil on canvas, 25-5/8 x 32 in. (65.2 x 81.2 cm). Collection of the Museum of Fine Arts, Boston. Juliana Cheney Edwards Collection. Bequest of Robert J. Edwards in memory of his mother, 1925

Georgia O'Keeffe (American, 1887–1986). *The Red Hills with Sun (Red Hills, Lake George)*, 1927.
Oil on canvas, 27 x 32 in. (68.6 x 81.3 cm). Copyright © The Phillips Collection, Washington, D.C.

Othon Friesz (French, 1879–1949). *Paysage (Le bec-de-l'aigle, La ciotat)* (Landscape [The Eagle's Beak, La Ciotat]), 1907. Oil on canvas, 25-3/8 x 32 in. (64.5 x 81.2 cm). Collection of the San Francisco Museum of Modern Art. Bequest of Marion W. Sinton. Photograph: Don Myer

Alfred Stieglitz (American, 1864–1946). *Equivalent*, 1929. Gelatin silver print, 4-2/3 x 3-2/3 in.
(11.9 x 9.2 cm). Collection of the Victoria and Albert Museum, London

Vincent van Gogh (Dutch, worked in France, 1853–1890). *The Flowering Orchard*, 1888. Oil on canvas, 28-1/2 x 21 in. (72.4 x 53.3 cm). Collection of The Metropolitan Museum of Art, New York. Mr. and Mrs. Henry Ittleson, Jr., Fund, 1956

Man Ray (American, 1890–1976) *Hills*, 1914. Oil on canvas, 10-1/8 x 12 in. (25.7 x 30.5 cm).
Collection of the Munson-Williams-Proctor Institute, Utica, New York

Maurice de Vlaminck (French, 1876–1958). *Route maraichère* (Road to the Garden Market), 1907.
Oil on canvas, 23-1/8 x 28-1/4 in. (60 x 73 cm). Collection of the Kunstmuseum Winterthur, Volkart
Stiftung, Winterthur, Switzerland

Charles Burchfield (American, 1893–1967). *Afternoon in the Grove,* July 11, 1916. Watercolor with pencil on paper, 14 x 20 in. (35.6 x 50.8 cm). Collection of the Burchfield Art Center, Buffalo State College, New York. Gift of Tony Sisti, 1979. Photograph: Henrich Photographs

Vincent van Gogh (Dutch, worked in France, 1853–1890). *The Mulberry Tree*, 1889. Oil on canvas, 21-1/4 x 25-1/2 in. (54 x 65 cm). Collection of the Norton Simon Art Foundation, Pasadena, California

Arthur Dove (American, 1880–1946) *Wooded Pond*, 1935. Watercolor on paper, 5 x 7 in. (12.7 x 17.8 cm)
The Phillips Collection, Washington, D.C.

Bernard Perlin (American, b. 1918). *The Farewell*, 1952. Casein on fiberboard, 34-1/8 x 47-1/8 in. (86.7 x 119.7 cm). Collection of the National Museum of American Art, Smithsonian Institution, Washington, D.C. Sara Roby Foundation Collection. Photograph: Courtesy Art Resource, New York

Charles Burchfield (American, 1893–1967). *Winter Landscape with Trees*, 1916. Watercolor on paper, 11 x 20 in. (27.9 x 50.8 cm). Collection of the Kennedy Galleries, Inc., New York

Albert Renger-Patzsch (German, 1897–1966). *Buchenwald im Herbst*, 1936. Gelatin silver print, 9 x 6-5/8 in. (22.8 x 16.8 cm). Collection of The Metropolitan Museum of Art, New York. Warner Communications Inc., Purchase Fund, 1978.602.1

Thomas P. Anshutz (American, 1851–1912). *Landscape*, n.d. Watercolor on cardboard, 10 x 12 in. (25.4 x 30.5 cm). Courtesy of The Pennsylvania Academy of the Fine Arts, Philadelphia. Gift of Mrs. Edward Anshutz

Charles Burchfield (American, 1893–1967). *Landscape with Trees*, 1915. Watercolor on paper, 10 x 14 in. (25.4 x 35.6 cm). Collection of the Kennedy Galleries, Inc., New York

Marsden Hartley (American, 1877–1943). *Storm Clouds, Maine*, 1906–7. Oil on canvas, 30-1/8 x 24-15/16 in. (76.5 x 63.4 cm). Collection of the Walker Art Center, Minneapolis. Gift of the T.B. Walker Foundation, Hudson Walker Collection, 1954

André Derain (French, 1880–1954). *Les Arbres* (The Trees), c. 1906. Oil on canvas, 23-3/8 x 28-1/2 in. (59.4 x 72.4 cm). Collection of the Albright-Knox Art Gallery, Buffalo, New York. Gift of Seymour H. Knox in memory of Helen Northrup Knox, 1971

Wolf Kahn (American, b. 1927). *Autumn River*, 1979. Oil on canvas, 52 x 72 in. (132.1 x 182.9 cm). Collection of The Metropolitan Museum of Art, New York. Purchase, The Martin S. Ackerman Foundation Gift, 1979

Charles Burchfield (American, 1893–1967). *Landscape with Rain*, 1917. Watercolor on paper, 13-1/2
x 19-1/2 in. (34.3 x 49.5 cm). Collection of the Kennedy Galleries, Inc., New York

Arthur Dove (American, 1880–1946). *Red Sun*, 1935. Oil on canvas, 20-1/4 x 28 in. (51.5 x 71.1 cm).
The Phillips Collection, Washington, D.C.

Marsden Hartley (American, 1877–1943). *Roses*, 1943. Oil on canvas, 40 x 30-1/8 in. (101.6 x 76.5 cm).
Collection of the Walker Art Center, Minneapolis. Gift of Ione and Hudson D. Walker, 1971

Vincent van Gogh (Dutch, worked in France, 1853–1890). *The Starry Night*, 1889. Oil on canvas, 29 x 36-1/4 in. (73.7 x 92.1 cm). Collection, The Museum of Modern Art, New York. Acquired through the Lillie P. Bliss Bequest

Selected Biography

Robert Frost was born March 26, 1874, in San Francisco. He moved to Lawrence, Massachusetts, at age eleven, and spent the remainder of his life — except for a brief period in England from 1912–15 — in the New England area. Although he never completed college, he briefly attended Dartmouth in 1892 and Harvard University from 1897–99. In 1895 Frost married Elinor Miriam White, with whom he had six children (two of whom died at early ages). Experiencing difficulties earning a living, he moved with his wife to a farm in Derry, New Hampshire, where Frost worked as a chicken farmer for ten years (1900–10) before sailing to England in 1912. It was in England that Frost's first books were published: *A Boy's Will* (1913) and *North of Boston* (1914).

Frost returned to America in 1915 as an established poet, where, over the course of his life, he would complete fifteen books in all (four of which earned Pulitzer Prizes). A lecturer and poet-in-residence at universities including Amherst College, Harvard, University of Michigan, and Dartmouth, Frost received a number of honorary degrees as well as awards. In 1962 he was awarded a Congressional gold metal and in 1963 a Bollingen Prize. He died in Boston on January 29, 1963, at the age of 88.